Psalms for
the Highs
and Lows
of Life

MEETING
GOD

Interactions Small Group Series

Authenticity: Being Honest with God and Others
Character: Reclaiming Six Endangered Qualities
Commitment: Developing Deeper Devotion to Christ
Community: Building Relationships within God's Family
Essential Christianity: Practical Steps for Spiritual Growth
Fruit of the Spirit: Living the Supernatural Life
Getting a Grip: Finding Balance in Your Daily Life
Jesus: Seeing Him More Clearly
Lessons on Love: Building Deeper Relationships
Living in God's Power: Finding God's Strength for Life's Challenges
Love in Action: Experiencing the Joy of Serving
Marriage: Building Real Intimacy
Meeting God: Psalms for the Highs and Lows of Life
New Identity: Discovering Who You Are in Christ
Parenting: How to Raise Spiritually Healthy Kids
Prayer: Opening Your Heart to God
Reaching Out: Sharing God's Love Naturally
The Real Deal: Discover the Rewards of Authentic Relationships
Significance: Understanding God's Purpose for Your Life
Transformation: Letting God Change You from the Inside Out

InterActions
small group series

Psalms for
the Highs
and Lows
of Life

MEETING
GOD

Previously published as *Psalms*

BILL HYBELS
WITH KEVIN AND SHERRY HARNEY

ZONDERVAN™

GRAND RAPIDS, MICHIGAN 49530 USA

WILLOW
Willow Creek Resources

We want to hear from you. Please send your comments about this book to us in care of zreview@zondervan.com. Thank you.

ZONDERVAN™

Meeting God
Copyright © 1997 by Willow Creek Association
Previously published as *Psalms*

Requests for information should be addressed to:

Zondervan, *Grand Rapids, Michigan 49530*

ISBN-10: 0-310-26599-1
ISBN-13: 978-0-310-26599-3

Interior design by Rick Devon and Michelle Espinoza

Printed in the United States of America

05 06 07 08 09 10 11 12 /❖ DCI/ 10 9 8 7 6 5 4 3 2 1

CONTENTS

INTERACTIONS

In 1992, Willow Creek Community Church, in partnership with Zondervan and the Willow Creek Association, released a curriculum for small groups entitled the Walking with God series. In just three years, almost a half million copies of these small group study guides were being used in churches around the world. The phenomenal response to this curriculum affirmed the need for relevant and biblical small group materials.

At the writing of this curriculum, there are nearly 3,000 small groups meeting regularly within the structure of Willow Creek Community Church. We believe this number will increase as we continue to place a central value on small groups. Many other churches throughout the world are growing in their commitment to small group ministries as well, so the need for resources is increasing.

In response to this great need, the Interactions small group series has been developed. Willow Creek Association and Zondervan have joined together to create a whole new approach to small group materials. These discussion guides are meant to challenge group members to a deeper level of sharing, to create lines of accountability, to move followers of Christ into action, and to help group members become fully devoted followers of Christ.

SUGGESTIONS FOR INDIVIDUAL STUDY

1. Begin each session with prayer. Ask God to help you understand the passage and to apply it to your life.
2. A good modern translation, such as the New International Version, the New American Standard Bible, or the New Revised Standard Version, will give you the most help. Questions in this guide are based on the New International Version.
3. Read and reread the passage(s). You must know what the passage says before you can understand what it means and how it applies to you.
4. Write your answers in the spaces provided in the study guide. This will help you to express clearly your understanding of the passage.
5. Keep a Bible dictionary handy. Use it to look up unfamiliar words, names, or places.

SUGGESTIONS FOR GROUP STUDY

1. Come to the session prepared. Careful preparation will greatly enrich your time in group discussion.
2. Be willing to join in the discussion. The leader of the group will not be lecturing, but will encourage people to discuss what they have learned in the passage. Plan to share what God has taught you in your individual study.
3. Stick to the passage being studied. Base your answers on the verses being discussed rather than on outside authorities such as commentaries or your favorite author or speaker.
4. Try to be sensitive to the other members of the group. Listen attentively when they speak, and be affirming whenever you can. This will encourage more hesitant members of the group to participate.
5. Be careful not to dominate the discussion. By all means participate, but allow others to have equal time.
6. If you are the discussion leader, you will find additional suggestions and helpful ideas in the leader's notes.

ADDITIONAL RESOURCES AND TEACHING MATERIALS

At the end of this study guide you will find a collection of resources and teaching materials to help you in your growth as a follower of Christ. You will also find resources that will help your church develop and build fully devoted followers of Christ.

Introduction: Psalms for the Highs and Lows of Life

Throughout the centuries, God's people have sung about their faith, writing tens of thousands of songs. Some songs are joy-filled explosions of exaltation and praise. Some are popular for a short time; others, such as "Amazing Grace" and "Great Is Thy Faithfulness," have become classics sung on many continents, in many languages, and over many years. Still others record the great things God has done. Many are prayers of humble confession. Often these songs declare who God is and remind us of His character and promises.

Of all the worship songs ever written, the book of the Bible known as Psalms is the most famous. This collection of 150 songs has given inspiration to the people of God for thousands of years! The messages found in the psalms are very similar to those found in our modern-day hymns and praise choruses: they express profound joy as well as deep sorrow, honest declarations of trust as well as heart-wrenching cries of lament. But no matter what theme each psalm contains, reading them helps us deepen our relationship with God. They challenge us to trust God, to walk in obedience, to lift our hearts in worship, and to live with confidence and hope. Listen to the words of the psalmist:

> Shout for joy to the LORD, all the earth.
> Worship the LORD with gladness;
> come before him with joyful songs.
> Know that the LORD is God.
> It is he who made us, and we are his;
> we are his people, the sheep of his pasture.
> Enter his gates with thanksgiving
> and his courts with praise;
> give thanks to him and praise his name.
> For the LORD is good and his love endures forever;
> his faithfulness continues through all generations.
>
> *PSALM 100*

Let the message of the psalms capture your heart and fill you with expressions of gratitude, worship, and hope.

THE ROAD TO BLESSEDNESS

THE BIG PICTURE

Every year fortune-tellers and soothsayers try to predict what will happen in the coming year. Right now the hot term is "psychic." We don't hear about fortune-telling or palm reading nearly as much, but psychics are big business. There are many "dial-a-psychic" commercials on television inviting us to discover what our future holds—for a fee. People readily shell out their hard-earned money looking for any way to gain insight to their future.

Over time, most of us learn that nobody can accurately predict future events. As much as people might want channelers, gurus, or psychics to give them a window to the future, it simply does not happen.

It is this human interest in figuring out the future that causes us to raise an eyebrow when we read Psalm 1. It seems the psalmist is telling us he can peek into our future. With authority, he tells us some interesting things about what is going to happen up the road. He says he can predict the future blessedness quotient of what we will experience in our life. He knows that some people will experience deep satisfaction of the soul while others will face barrenness in their heart and life.

A WIDE ANGLE VIEW

1 Why is there such a deep desire in the human spirit to know the future?

Do you have a friend or relative for whom this is a preoccupation? How does this preoccupation affect their life?

A BIBLICAL PORTRAIT

Read Psalm 1

2 In verses 1–3 the psalmist paints a picture of a person who will experience "blessedness." What characteristics mark this person's life?

3

What do we learn about the future of the "wicked" from this psalm?

What contrast do you see between these two pictures?

SHARPENING THE FOCUS

Read Snapshot "Blessedness"

BLESSEDNESS

What is blessedness? As the Bible describes it, blessedness is the heart condition for which the whole world is looking. It is an indescribable inner sense of well-being and dignity, a calm assurance of self-worth. It is that vitality of spirit that you feel when you know deep down in the core of your being that you are rightly related to God. There are no obstacles between you and Him; you can feel and sense His presence and activity in your life.

Blessedness is knowing that over time you are being conformed to His image. It is knowing that you are being used regularly for God's purposes, and that your life matters to Him. Blessedness is knowing that God is pleased, not only with who you are, but with what you are doing with your life. It is knowing that God is providing individual protection, care, and guidance for you, that He is going to take you home with Him someday and you are going to spend eternity with Him. Blessedness is that rock-solid confidence that God is in control of your life . . . even in the middle of storms and trials.

> *Blessed is the man*
> *who does not walk in the counsel of the wicked*
> *or stand in the way of sinners*
> *or sit in the seat of mockers.*
> *But his delight is in the law of the LORD,*
> *and on his law he meditates day and night.*
> *He is like a tree planted by streams of water,*
> *which yields its fruit in season*
> *and whose leaf does not wither.*
> *Whatever he does prospers.*
>
> PSALM 1:1–3

4 What are some sources of advice or counsel you need to avoid?

5 What do you think is involved in keeping yourself by God's streams of water?

How can your small group members encourage you and keep you accountable to spend time in God's Word?

6 What fruit do you see growing in your life at this time?

Read Snapshot "Barrenness"

BARRENNESS

The psalmist predicts that certain people face a grim, dark future. These "barren" people will be filled with the gnawing absence of any sense of peace with God. They will be continually confused as to what the game of life is all about. People who live for the things of this world will not discover the meaning of life. They will have a growing fear of death and whatever follows it. The psalmist refers to these people as the "wicked." They are like chaff which the wind drives away. All of their efforts are futile, their lives meaningless. Even though they hunger for blessing, all they feel is barrenness.

Not so the wicked!
They are like chaff
that the wind blows away.
Therefore the wicked will not stand in the judgment,
nor sinners in the assembly of the righteous.

PSALM 1:4—5

---

7 If you have experienced true blessedness from God, what would you say to a person who is still trapped in a barren life?

8 Think of a friend or family member who is living a barren life. How might you bring this person the message that God wants them to experience His blessedness?

Read Snapshot "The Road to Blessedness . . . Obedience"

THE ROAD TO BLESSEDNESS . . . OBEDIENCE

The psalmist says that only the road named "obedience" will lead to true blessedness. God clearly outlines a map for us to follow. His Word, the Bible, points the direction to faith in Jesus Christ and right living. God gives us the Holy Spirit to encourage us to walk the road of obedience as well as brothers and sisters in faith to support us on the way. If we follow this road, we will ultimately be overwhelmed by how much blessedness He will pour into our life.

9 What is one area in your life in which you have been wandering off the road of obedience?

What can your group members do to help you stay on the path?

PUTTING YOURSELF IN THE PICTURE

DELIGHTING IN GOD'S WORD

The psalmist tells us that one of the things that will help us experience a blessed life is delighting in God's law and meditating on His Word day and night. Take time in the coming week to memorize and meditate on the first three verses of Psalm 1.

WALKING THE ROAD OF BLESSEDNESS

Identify one specific area in your life where you are not being obedient to God. Do the following things to help you walk the road of obedience in this area:

- Confess your disobedience and ask for a deep understanding of God's forgiveness.
- Be specific about what it will mean to walk in obedience in this area of your life. What actions must start or stop?
- Pray for the presence and power of the Holy Spirit to fill you as you seek to follow God in this area of your life.
- Ask a close Christian brother or sister to pray for you and keep you accountable to stay on the road of obedience.

PEOPLE MATTER TO GOD

REFLECTIONS FROM SESSION 1

1. How has meditating on Psalm 1:1–3 deepened your understanding of blessedness?
2. What changes have occurred in your life since your last meeting because of your commitment to walk in obedience to God?

THE BIG PICTURE

Have you ever been in an airplane cruising over a major metropolitan area at an altitude of 35,000–40,000 feet? If you have, there is a good chance you have looked out the window and been struck by how small things look from that vantage point. A whole city looks about the size of a postage stamp. As you gain this "heavenly" perspective, it almost feels like you could reach down, pick up that little postage stamp, crinkle it up, and blow it out of your hand. Who would even care? Distance changes our whole perspective, doesn't it?

David looked into the infinite expanses of space and acknowledged the human tendency to wonder about our value in light of the whole created order. As he considered the size, splendor, and magnitude of the created realm, his natural response was to say, "What are people? We are so small, fragile, and insignificant in comparison to the rest of creation." Who wants to mess with mere men and women? How could God even notice such little creatures? And His perspective is much higher than just 35,000 feet!

Most of us have faced the sobering sadness of feeling like a miniature nobody. Almost all of us have faced times in our lives when we wondered if we really mattered to God, when we say, "Who am I? I'm just a speck of dust. A blip on the radar screen. A single grain of sand in the Sahara Desert." When we consider the magnitude of the created realm, how can we feel anything but small and insignificant?

A WIDE ANGLE VIEW

1 Describe a time you had a sense of the vastness of creation. How did this make you feel about yourself in relationship to the created order?

A BIBLICAL PORTRAIT

Read Psalm 8

2 What does this psalm teach us about:

- The heavens and the earth

- The God we follow

3 How does David portray human beings:

- In verse 4

- In verses 5–8

How do these two portraits fit together?

SHARPENING THE FOCUS

Read Snapshot "Made in the Image of God"

MADE IN THE IMAGE OF GOD

In Genesis 1:26 God says, "Let us make man in our image, in our likeness, and let them rule over the fish of the sea and the birds of the air, over the livestock, over all the earth, and over all the creatures that move along the ground." When God had finished all the rest of His creation, on the sixth day, it is as though He rolled up His sleeves and said, "Now, for the finale I am going to create something distinct. I am going to really show my stuff. I am going to create a man and a woman who will bear My image."

You see, human beings alone are created in the image of God. We are entirely different than anything else in the created realm. When God made us He created an expression of Himself. The implications of being created in God's image are staggering. If you wonder how much you matter to God, wonder no longer. You are His unique creation, made in His image.

4 What does it mean to be made in the image of God?

5 Since every human being is created in God's image, how should this reality impact *one* of these areas:

- How we treat non-Christians
- How we respond to racism
- How we view ourselves

Read Snapshot "God Shows No Partiality"

GOD SHOWS NO PARTIALITY

Psalm 8 gives proof of our special significance to God. Of all the things in creation, He says that we are His favorite. Human beings are the pinnacle of all God has made. At the same time, we can have confidence that we matter to God every bit as much as any other human being. The Bible says repeatedly that God is no respecter of persons. There is absolutely no partiality with Him. Each of us is made in His image, carries some of His attributes, has a soul that yearns to be rightly related to Him, is capable of being redeemed, and is called to join His mission of reconciling others. And each of us is going to live forever in His presence.

6 What are some of the things that make us feel less important than others?

How can we battle against these lies?

7 What can you do to build up others and affirm their value as human beings?

Read Snapshot "God Gives Us Responsibility"

GOD GIVES US RESPONSIBILITY

Human beings alone are given dominion over God's creation. God has called us to be the stewards of the world He has made. That He has given human beings responsibility is graphically portrayed in the book of Genesis when Adam and Eve are called to care for the earth, to till and keep it. Think about that. How many people would you allow to live in your home for a month while you are out of town? What kind of person would you trust that much? We matter to God so much that He gave us responsibility to care for His creation.

8 What is a responsibility God has given you in *one* of these areas:

- Using a spiritual gift to do ministry
- Caring for a person
- Supervising material resources
- Some other responsibility

How does having this responsibility remind you how much you matter to God?

PUTTING YOURSELF IN THE PICTURE

Seeing People Through the Eyes of God

Take time in the coming week for honest and tough self-examination. Are there groups of people you feel don't matter to God as much as others do? Do you discriminate on the basis of skin color, ethnic background, gender, economic standing, or any other grounds? If you do, confess this and pray for eyes to see people the way God does.

Remember that you are just as important to God as anyone else is. At the same time, every other person matters to God as much as you do. Pray for a new heart of love for every person, because each is made in the image of God.

Living Responsibly

God gives us all responsibilities. As a follower of Christ, you are called to live for Him. Identify one area in your life in which God has given you a responsibility to live for Him but in which you have not been fulfilling that responsibility. Renew your efforts to live responsibly for God. Pray for a deeper sense of how much you matter to Him as you do the work He has given. Remember, God gives responsibility to those He trusts.

Area in which I need to renew responsible living:

Specific actions I need to change:

Person who will pray for me and support me along the way:

REASONS FOR PRAISE

REFLECTIONS FROM SESSION 2

1. If God has given you new eyes to see how much people matter to Him, how is this impacting your relationships?
2. How have you been growing in responsible living? How has this deepened your understanding that you matter to God?

THE BIG PICTURE

It is amazing to discover how many people we know who have had a close brush with death. Some people have been in car accidents that could have easily cost them their lives. Others have had an illness that took them to the doorstep of death. And there are many who have been in battle during wartime and faced death on a daily basis.

If you have faced death, or even the possibility of death, you know it is an experience a person never forgets. The details stay fresh in your mind, and the memories come back when you think about the incident. These memories are often in living color . . . as vivid as if they had happened yesterday. Sometimes you can even remember the sounds and smells associated with the event, the looks on people's faces, the terror. When you think back to that close call, you usually breathe a sigh of relief once again and thank God for the miracle of His protection.

David had numerous brushes with death. Not only did he face lions and bears in the wilderness as he took care of his father's flock, but he also dodged spears that King Saul threw at him in a jealous rage. One time, when David was on the run because Saul wanted him dead, he hid out in a city called Gath. A rumor started floating around the city that David had come there with plans for a military takeover. David was trapped in the city when he got word that King Abimelech, the city's ruler, wanted him dead. Because David feared for his life, he did a very unusual thing to try to escape the city—he acted insane, throwing himself against the gates of the city and foaming at the mouth. The king saw David and said to his counselors, "Is this the person you say is a threat to my throne? Ha! Ha! He is no threat to me. Let him go. I don't need any more madmen in this city." Once again, David had a close brush with death but was spared.

A WIDE ANGLE VIEW

1 Tell about an experience you had where you (or someone close to you) could have died.

How did you feel when you (or they) were spared?

A BIBLICAL PORTRAIT

Read Psalm 34

2 This psalm identifies many reasons for giving praise to God. What are one or two of the reasons listed in this psalm that move you to praise?

3 This psalm was written by David after he pretended to be insane and barely escaped with his life from Abimelech, the King of Gath. With this context in mind, how does this psalm communicate the heart of a person who just had a brush with death?

SHARPENING THE FOCUS

Read Snapshot "An Explosion of Exaltation"

AN EXPLOSION OF EXALTATION

At the beginning of this psalm, David, his heart bursting with adoration for God, erupts in an explosion of praise. But like most true worshipers, David has a sense that he wants to express his worship in a deeper way. He feels God deserves more than he can give with his own songs, praise, and exaltation.

David has a partial solution for his feelings of inadequacy. He expresses his desire for all believers everywhere to come and magnify the Lord together. He invites everyone to join him in this expression of worship. It is as if he feels that when we join our voices together, we can more fully express praise to God. As one song writer put it, "Oh for a thousand tongues to sing, my great Redeemer's praise." David is saying the same thing. He wants everyone to join him in a corporate explosion of exaltation to God!

> I will extol the LORD at all times;
> his praise will always be on my lips.
> My soul will boast in the LORD;
> let the afflicted hear and rejoice.
> Glorify the LORD with me;
> let us exalt his name together.
>
> PSALM 34:1–3

4 What life situations bring you to a point where you are moved to a deep expression of praise?

5 There are many ways to express exaltation. The Bible talks about singing, playing instruments, shouting, dancing, writing psalms, and many other forms of expression. What helps you express worship?

What psalm, hymn, or praise song helps you express your feelings of worship to God?

Read Snapshot "The Power of Personal Faith"

THE POWER OF PERSONAL FAITH

In this psalm David praises God for the power he experienced in his personal and intimate relationship with Him. God was not some far-off deity; David had cried out to God and had received an answer! He knew the deliverance and presence of God, and his heart was filled with praise.

There is really no substitute for personal, firsthand, private, faith experiences with Jesus. You will never build confidence in God by simply wishing for it, by studying religious data, or by listening to other people describe how God delivered them. You build personal faith in God when you cry out to the Lord, venture out on a limb of faith, and personally follow the leading of the Holy Spirit. When it is just you and the Lord in the furnace of life, faith grows real.

I sought the LORD, and he answered me;
he delivered me from all my fears.
Those who look to him are radiant;
their faces are never covered with shame.
This poor man called, and the LORD heard him;
he saved him out of all his troubles.
The angel of the LORD encamps around those who fear him,
and he delivers them.

PSALM 34:4–7

6 Describe a time when God was the only One you could turn to . . . when He became your lifeline. How did this experience deepen your personal faith?

How does looking back on this experience create within you
an attitude of gratitude?

7 Where do you need God to deliver you and encircle you with the protection of His angels?

In what ways can your small group members pray for you and support you in this area?

Read Snapshot "An Invitation to Anyone"

AN INVITATION TO ANYONE

David gives an invitation to anyone who will listen to him. He says, "Taste and see that the LORD is good." This is one of the most famous verses in the whole book of Psalms. It is as if David is saying, "I can tell you about God's goodness. Other people can tell you. You can read about it. You can sing about it. But there comes a time when you have to taste personally and see that God is good beyond your wildest dreams."

We need to learn from David's boldness. We need to say to people, "You think what you have is better than what Christ can give you, but you're wrong. God can give you so much more than what you are clutching in your arms. God may ask you to give something up, but whatever it is isn't good for you anyway." We need to start inviting others to come and taste God's goodness.

Taste and see that the LORD is good;
blessed is the man who takes refuge in him.
PSALM 34:8

8 Suppose a seeker looked you straight in the eye and said, "I don't believe all this talk about how good it is to be a Christian. Why don't you tell me, from your personal experience, how God has shown His goodness to you." What would you say?

9 How can you extend the invitation "Taste and see that the Lord is good" to a specific person in your life?

PUTTING YOURSELF IN THE PICTURE

AN EXPLOSION OF EXALTATION

Sit down and write one full page of praise and exaltation to God. Try to fill the whole page with words of worship, sentences of praise, and expressions of exaltation. Try to remember what God has done for you in the past, what He is doing now, and what He has promised for your future. Let your words and worship explode from your heart and spill over onto the page.

When you are done, read this page out loud with heart-felt expression. If you dare, call one of your small group members and read it to that person. Let your praise inspire him or her to openly express exaltation to God as well.

EXTENDING THE INVITATION

If you have tasted and experienced the goodness of God, invite someone else to come to the table. Consider this question: When you eat at a great restaurant and have a superior meal, what do you do? Most likely, over the next few days, you tell someone about it. "The appetizers were incredible! The steak melted in my mouth! The service was fantastic! The desserts were out of this world!" No one finds it strange to tell others about a great meal.

If you are a follower of Christ and have dined at the table of His goodness, you too have news to tell. Identify a person in your life who has not yet experienced the delicacies of God's goodness. Tell that person, from your personal experience, how you have feasted on God's goodness and how wonderful it is. Then, invite him or her to the table. Remember, you don't have to make the meal—that's God's job. You are only called to invite people to His table.

GOD ONLY

REFLECTIONS FROM SESSION 3

1. If you are comfortable doing so, read some of your "explosion of exaltation" notes. Or tell your group one or two things that has moved your heart to praise.
2. If you told someone about God's goodness this week and invited them to "Taste and see that the Lord is good," how did they respond?

THE BIG PICTURE

When I was very young, I burned up an expensive farm tractor. I had been carefully instructed on many occasions to never fill the tractor with gasoline while the motor was still hot, but I was in a hurry one day and didn't take time to let the motor cool off. As I filled the tank with gasoline, some of it spilled. The tractor caught on fire and was completely destroyed. Because of this incident, I discovered at a young age that there are some lessons in life you learn the hard way!

Then, when I was a teenager, I almost killed myself and a friend in an airplane. Beginning with the first flying lesson I had taken, my instructor had taught me to always do a preflight inspection. He said, "The first thing you do, before you even think about getting into the plane, is to slowly walk around the plane and give it a preflight. Check all the little pins. Check the oil. Be sure to tighten the fuel caps yourself." I did a rigorous preflight inspection before every flight . . . until I got my license.

Once I was licensed, my preflight inspection time diminished rapidly. It wasn't long before I would just go to the hangar, kick the tire, get in, and start it up. One night I was going to take a friend out flying. We needed fuel, so I pulled up to the pumps. When I went in to check the weather I noticed a very responsible looking junior high student filling up the gas tanks in the plane. I asked the kid, "Is it all set?" With confidence he said, "It's all set!"

In order for me to have inspected the tanks visually, I would have had to take a stepladder out and climbed up on the plane. Instead of doing this, I trusted the word of the young man who filled the plane's tanks. We took off and went flying over Chicago. As we were heading back, I looked at the fuel gauge. It should have still been on full, but it was almost on empty. I knew we were in big trouble. I looked over my shoulder and saw a film of gasoline streaming down the rear of the cockpit. Immediately, I knew what had happened. That "responsible looking" junior high boy had forgotten to put on the fuel caps.

My heart started racing, but I tried to stay cool. We landed on fumes, but we landed safely. As I was putting the plane away, I peeked up on the wing. Sure enough, there lay both fuel caps on the back of the wing, hanging only by their safety chains.

Ever since that night I always check the fuel caps and do a complete preflight inspection. Even when I am flying with someone else, I try to get a look at the fuel caps. When I fly a major airline, I sometimes find myself wishing I could walk around the plane, do a preflight inspection and personally tighten the fuel caps. I learned my lesson the hard way, but I did learn my lesson!

A WIDE ANGLE VIEW

1 What is one life lesson you learned the hard way?

Read Psalm 62

2 In this psalm we find statements like "in God alone" and "He alone." What does this psalm teach about what "God alone" offers?

3 In verses 9–12 we read warnings and promises. Put these in your own words:

- Warnings:

- Promises:

Read Snapshot "God Only"

GOD ONLY

As I read Psalm 62 the recurring theme of "God only" jumps out at me. In this psalm, David has a powerful message for all who will listen. Throughout his life, David has come to experience that only God can be his protection in a harsh world. When weary, tired, and at the end of his rope, he has discovered that the only place to find rest for his soul is in God. He has learned that in a hopeless situation, only God brings hope.

Do you start to get the point? In a world that offers countless options for where we can focus our attention, David gives us an example of being sold out for God. The model of his life acts as an invitation for us to be "God only" men and women . . . fully devoted followers of Christ who are completely committed to God alone.

---

4 What marks the lives of the "God only" Christians you know?

5 What is standing in the way of you being more of a "God only" follower of Christ?

What is it going to take to tear down these barriers?

38

6 What can you do as a small group to challenge and inspire each other to be "God only" people?

Read Snapshot "God and . . ."

GOD AND . . .

After his fairy-tale ascent to national stardom, David slowly slipped from being a "God only" man to a "God and" man. A "God and" person is someone who tries to please God *and* people at the same time. He or she is someone who attempts to lay up treasures in heaven *and* build an impressive portfolio here on earth. A "God and" person wants the full blessing of God *and* the pleasures of sin. He or she wants what God wants *and* what they want too. "God and" people have one foot in God's canoe and another foot in the world's canoe. This kind of person fudges, hedges, and rationalizes in order to perpetuate this chameleon-like charade.

What complicates the matter is that a "God and" person isn't obedient enough to be greatly used by God, but isn't wicked enough to throw caution to the wind and join the dance with demons. He or she misses the joys of serving Christ but never thoroughly drowns in the folly of sin. They are caught in the middle—no heavenly thrills, no hellish spills. This is not an easy way to live the Christian life.

7 What are some of the dangers and consequences of living a "God and" life?

8 What is one area you are presently living a "God and" life?

How can your group members support you as you seek to reject a "God and" lifestyle and adopt a "God only" lifestyle in this area?

PUTTING YOURSELF IN THE PICTURE

"IN GOD ALONE"

Take time in the coming week to memorize and reflect on four verses from Psalm 62. Each verse highlights the need for us to be "God only" people:

> My soul finds rest in God alone;
> my salvation comes from him.
> He alone is my rock and my salvation;
> he is my fortress, I will never be shaken. . . .
> Find rest, O my soul, in God alone;
> my hope comes from him.
> He alone is my rock and my salvation;
> he is my fortress, I will not be shaken.
> *PSALM 62:1–2 AND 5–6*

A JOURNEY FROM "GOD AND" TO "GOD ONLY"

In your small group study you identified one specific area in which you need to move from being a "God and" person to being a "God only" person. Commit yourself to do the following things as you seek to move from where you are to where God wants you to be.

- Honestly confess to God where you have become a "God and" person. Don't try to hide it or deny it.
- Identify what actions and attitudes are going to have to stop if you are going to become a "God only" person in this area.
- Identify specific actions that will need to begin as you journey toward being a "God only" follower of Christ.
- Seek prayer support and accountability from Christian brothers and sisters whom you trust.

- Look back on a regular basis and see how your life is changing. Make note of how you are surrendering more and more of your life to God. It might be helpful to get a journal and keep notes on the transformation that is happening in your life as you make this journey from being a "God and" person to becoming a "God only" person.

FREEDOM FROM FEAR

REFLECTIONS FROM SESSION 4

1. How has memorizing Psalm 62:1–2 and 5–6 deepened your commitment to be a "God only" person?
2. Describe the journey you are taking to move from being a "God and" person to being a "God only" person.

THE BIG PICTURE

Virtually no one is a stranger to fear. In fact, I heard a psychologist once say there are only two kinds of people who are exempt from having to deal with fear: dead people and deranged people. All the rest of us find ourselves dealing with fear more often than we would like to admit.

Some of us deal with annoying little minor-league fears. I have a friend who says, "It's not the sharks that get me, it's the guppies." He is talking about those *pestering fears* that keep nagging at us. Will the commission check cover the cost of my new golf clubs? Will my dinner turn out right for my guests? Will my client sign on for another year? Will the kids do well on their final exams? These pestering fears take more of a toll on us than we realize. But if all we had to deal with in life were these kinds of little fears, we would probably manage quite nicely.

However, if we add just one or two *pressing fears* to our pestering fears, then our ship starts taking on some water. These are major-league fears that arise from real-life struggles that can face any of us. For example, you hear rumors floating around your company that there is a restructuring on the horizon and you are probably going to lose your job. You get a call from the high school counselor informing you that your child is having severe problems and his grades are falling. You see an important relationship in your life breaking up and you feel there is nothing you can do about it. Someone you love has a drinking problem and they are resisting help. These are all pressing fears. They can weigh us down and wreak havoc in our heads. They cause mild panic and drain our energy and vitality.

And then there is the still deeper *paralyzing fear*. This is an immobilizing, panic-producing fear that leads to feelings of stark terror. When we face a paralyzing fear, we freeze up, our pulse races, our throat gets dry, our hands get wet, our mind starts reeling, we become nauseous. This kind of fear sets in when you get news that you are facing a terminal illness or when a loved one suddenly dies. Paralyzing fear takes over when people receive an unexpected notice of termination at work or face a divorce or are confronted by a family crisis such as alcohol problems or sexual abuse. This kind of fear can destroy a life when it is not dealt with.

A WIDE ANGLE VIEW

1 How have you experienced *one* of these kinds of fear:
- A pestering fear
- A pressing fear
- A paralyzing fear

What is one fear you are facing right now?

A BIBLICAL PORTRAIT

Read Psalm 91

2 This psalm is filled with images and word pictures. What is one image that jumps out at you, and what does it teach you about God?

3 What message does this psalm speak to those who are struggling with fear?

SHARPENING THE FOCUS

Read Snapshot "Knowing Who God Is"

KNOWING WHO GOD IS

Psalm 91 has a message for those who are battling feelings of fear. The psalmist gives a number of reasons why those who love God can be free from the paralyzing power of fear. First, we can walk in faith because of who God is. The writer of this psalm asserts that he can travel through the minefields of life without caving in to fear because he is in a relationship with a God whose character, word, and direction can be trusted. The psalmist sees the might, power, and love of God with crystal clarity. He knows his God is a shelter, a protector, the Most High God!

4 What is one element of God's character that brings you courage and confidence?

How have you experienced freedom from fear because of this characteristic of God?

5 Describe a time you found yourself in a dangerous situation and God delivered you.

Read Snapshot "Surrounded by Angels"

SURROUNDED BY ANGELS

Second, the psalmist says he refuses to wander in the wastelands of fear because he knows he is protected by angels. Without apology, the psalmist lets us know that God will give His angels charge over us to guard us from evil. We don't talk about angels very much, but the Bible does. There are numerous passages about the ministry of angels. Do you want some relief from your fear? Remember that God has commissioned His angels to watch over you. Psalm 34:7 says, "The angel of the LORD encamps around those who fear him, and he delivers them." When you think you are exposed and vulnerable, remember, the angels of God are right there with you.

6 Tell about a time that you, or someone close to you, felt supernaturally protected.

7 If you picture angels surrounding you as you face a fearful situation, how might this change your fear level?

Read Snapshot "The Power of Prayer"

THE POWER OF PRAYER

Not only do we need to know who God is, not only do we need to realize that angels protect us, but we also need to exercise the power of prayer. The last three verses in Psalm 91 are clear: God hears the prayers of His children and He answers them. Read verse 15 slowly and reflect on what God says: "He will call upon me, and I will answer him; I will be with him in trouble, I will deliver him and honor him." God is reminding us that as we struggle and battle with fear, there is power in calling on His name in prayer.

Simply calling on the name of God can defuse fear. The apostle Paul says, "Do not be anxious about anything, but in everything, by prayer and petition, with thanksgiving, present your requests to God. And the peace of God, which transcends all understanding, will guard your hearts and your minds in Christ Jesus" (Phil. 4:6–7). In prayer, we give God the problem that is producing the fear. We must not just tell God about the problem; we must release it to Him and trust Him to watch over us.

8 Give an example of the difference between *telling God* about your fears and *releasing your fears to God* through prayer?

9 Tell about a time you released a fear to God through prayer and experienced His peace and freedom from fear.

PUTTING YOURSELF IN THE PICTURE

GETTING SERIOUS ABOUT PRAYER

Write out your prayers for one week. Focus specifically on praying about the areas in which you deal with fear. Writing your prayers will help because it is good to see the words right in front of you. Be careful to release your fears to God, not to just report the fears with which you are dealing. Here is an example of what a brief written prayer might look like:

> Lord, I am finding myself caving in to fear again this morning. Fear about my mother's health. Fear about my children's safety and future. Fear about future plans. But here and now, in Your very presence, I am deliberately choosing to bring You into my wasteland of fear. I release these fears to You. I recognize Your character, Your power, and Your protection, and I refuse to live alone in fear. I acknowledge that Your angels will watch over

me today. I let go of fear and take Your hand. Fill me with Your courage and confidence. In the name of Jesus, the One who destroyed the power of death and removes my fears. Amen.

GROWING IN THE KNOWLEDGE OF GOD

Read at least one chapter of Psalms each day until you finish this book of the Bible. Keep a notebook near your Bible and write down every time you learn something about the character of God. By the end of your study, you will have an enormous list of qualities and attributes of God that you learned from the psalms. You will also have a better grip on your fears as you learn more and more about the God who protects you and shelters you in the shadow of His wing.

THE GREATNESS OF GOD

REFLECTIONS FROM SESSION 5

1. How has releasing your fear to God in prayer helped you discover freedom from fear? If you have been writing down your prayers, how has this impacted your prayer life?
2. What have you learned about the character of God from your daily study of Psalms?

THE BIG PICTURE

Parents, grandparents, big brothers and sisters, aunts and uncles all know how dangerous it can be to introduce a child to a new experience. If you take a little child to a new ice cream parlor, teach her a fun new game, or introduce her to an enjoyable activity, you know what is going to happen. The response will almost certainly be, "Can we do it again?" "Can I have another scoop?" "Can we play this game every single night?" That's just the way kids are!

Most adults know what it is like to go on vacation after a long stretch of exhausting labor in their particular vocation. When you finally get to your vacation spot, you begin to unwind and enjoy yourself. After a day or two of getting away from the job, you start actually having an enjoyable time. You find yourself sitting by the pool, relaxing by the lake, skiing down a mountain, hoisting the sails on the boat, getting out on the golf course, or just reading a book. At this point, you are overcome by a strange realization. You let out a sigh of relief and say to yourself, "I could do this forever. I wish I could experience this indefinitely." Just like a little child we find our hearts crying out, "Can I do this every day?"

A WIDE ANGLE VIEW

1 Describe a time you had an "I could do this forever" feeling.

A BIBLICAL PORTRAIT

Read Psalm 145

2 After reflecting on Psalm 145, how do you think David would answer these questions:

What causes you to say, "I could do this forever"?

What is it about God's character that makes you praise Him?

3

What does this psalm teach us about:

- Who God is

- What God does

- How we should respond to God

SHARPENING THE FOCUS

Read Snapshot "The Greatness of God"

THE GREATNESS OF GOD

When David explodes in praise, he declares God's unsearchable and unfathomable greatness. This psalm reminds me of the famous childhood mealtime prayer: "God is great, God is good, let us thank Him for our food." There are alterations of that prayer, but most of the time they get the first three words right—"God is great!" What a fantastic truth to embed in the minds of little ones. David says God's greatness is so vast that words can't describe it, yet he still tries to express the greatness of God by describing His awesome works. It is as if David is saying, "Words can't contain the expanse of God's greatness, but just think of all He has done. Remember His works, His deeds, His mighty acts of power. We have a great God!"

Over the years, I have discovered that the most sincere and enthusiastic worshipers I know are the ones who understand the greatness of God. They don't stop at knowing God's greatness; they experience it in their own lives. They have learned that God still reveals His greatness through His character, through His mighty acts, and in the lives of His followers. God doesn't want us to settle for the historical greatness of Bible characters and those who have gone before us. God is still a great God and He wants to reveal that greatness in the lives of this generation of Christians.

4 How have you witnessed God's greatness in *one* of these areas:

- Creation
- In the life of a follower of Christ
- In the church

5 How have you seen God reveal His power and greatness in your life?

Read Snapshot "The Goodness of God"

THE GOODNESS OF GOD

God has an intrinsic inclination of goodness toward you and me that is bound up in the very identity of who He is. This is why Jesus explained the character of God in Matthew 7 by telling a story about fathers and children. He asked, "What kind of a father would give his son a stone if he asked for bread, or what kind of a caring parent would give their child a snake when they asked for a meal of fish? It would never happen. Would any good parent endanger the life of their child this way? Certainly not!" Then Jesus says, "If sin-stained human fathers have the ability to be good to their children, how much more will your perfect, holy heavenly Father be good to His children?" The answer is, more than we could ever dream.

I feel bad when I hear Christians say, "God has been very good to me, but I wonder when the other shoe will fall. I wonder when God is going to run out of His goodness." They don't understand that God's goodness is intrinsic to who He is.

6 What has God done to prove His goodness to you?

Do you ever place conditions on God's goodness, expecting
Him to be "good" in the exact way you want Him to be?

7

If God has proved His goodness over and over again,
why do we find ourselves waiting for His goodness to
run out?

Read Snapshot "The Glory of God"

THE GLORY OF GOD

David worships the Father for being a glorious God. About the only way I know how to help people understand what this means is to have them read Exodus 19:7–25. In this passage, God decided it was time for His people to get a glimpse of His glory. He told Moses that in three days He would pass by and let everyone receive a small fraction of His glory. God instructed the Israelites to wash their garments, pray, cleanse, and consecrate themselves in preparation for this event.

When the third day came, all the people gathered. God revealed a bit of His glory, graciously veiling it in a thick cloud because He knew the fullness of it would destroy them. At the moment God revealed His glory there was deafening thunder, lightning so bright it blinded the eyes, the sound of trumpets, the earth quaked, smoke and fire came from the mountain, the mountain itself shook violently, and God spoke in the thunder. There is only one word to describe the people's reaction to this event: terror.

8

How does getting glimpses of God's glory move you
to worship?

Read Snapshot "The Grace of God"

THE GRACE OF GOD

Grace is the mysterious, unpredictable propensity of God to take delight in bestowing benefits on undeserving people. God forgives the penitent, cleanses the sinners, and picks up those who fall. Then, because He is such an outrageously gracious God, chooses to use us again. David knew what it was to fall into the depths of sin. He also knew what it was to experience God's gracious forgiveness. When we can't lift our burdens any more, we realize how good it is that we serve an outrageously gracious God. He took our burdens on Himself and offers us the gracious gift of forgiveness of sins through Jesus Christ. That is grace.

9 In grace, God gives us gifts we do not deserve. What are some of the gifts of grace God has given to you?

10 What is one way you can declare and express your praise for God's greatness as an individual? As a small group?

PUTTING YOURSELF IN THE PICTURE

REFLECTING ON GOD'S GREATNESS

Take time in the coming week to memorize and reflect on Psalm 145:1–3. Let this become your prayer and declaration of praise:

I will exalt you, my God the King;
I will praise your name for ever and ever.
Every day I will praise you
and extol your name for ever and ever.
Great is the LORD and most worthy of praise;
his greatness no one can fathom.

PSALM 100

A PICTURE OF GRACE

Use the space provided below to create a list of the gifts God
has given you. Everything you have that you don't deserve is a
gift of His grace. Reflect on material things, spiritual blessings,
people in your life, joys you have experienced, and anything
else that comes to mind. Praise God for His amazing grace.
When you are feeling like you are being short-changed in life,
read this list and let it bring perspective. God's grace is beyond
measure.

LEADER'S NOTES

Leading a Bible discussion—especially for the first time—can make you feel both nervous and excited. If you are nervous, realize that you are in good company. Many biblical leaders, such as Moses, Joshua, and the apostle Paul, felt nervous and inadequate to lead others (see, for example, 1 Cor. 2:3). Yet God's grace was sufficient for them, just as it will be for you.

Some excitement is also natural. Your leadership is a gift to the others in the group. Keep in mind, however, that other group members also share responsibility for the group. Your role is simply to stimulate discussion by asking questions and encouraging people to respond. The suggestions listed below can help you to be an effective leader.

PREPARING TO LEAD

1. Ask God to help you understand and apply the passage to your own life. Unless that happens, you will not be prepared to lead others.
2. Carefully work through each question in the study guide. Meditate and reflect on the passage as you formulate your answers.
3. Familiarize yourself with the Leader's Notes for each session. These will help you understand the purpose of the session and will provide valuable information about the questions in the session. The Leader's Notes are not intended to be read to the group. These notes are primarily for your use as a group leader and for your preparation. However, when you find a section that relates well to your group, you may want to read a brief portion or encourage them to read this section at another time.
4. Pray for the various members of the group. Ask God to use these sessions to make you better disciples of Jesus Christ.
5. Before the first session, make sure each person has a study guide. Encourage them to prepare beforehand for each session.

LEADING THE SESSION

1. Begin the session on time. If people realize that the session begins on schedule, they will work harder to arrive on time.
2. At the beginning of your first time together, explain that these sessions are designed to be discussions, not lectures. Encourage everyone to participate, but realize some may be hesitant to speak during the first few sessions.
3. Don't be afraid of silence. People in the group may need time to think before responding.
4. Avoid answering your own questions. If necessary, rephrase a question until it is clearly understood. Even an eager group will quickly become passive and silent if they think the leader will do most of the talking.
5. Encourage more than one answer to each question. Ask, "What do the rest of you think?" or "Anyone else?" until several people have had a chance to respond.
6. Try to be affirming whenever possible. Let people know you appreciate their insights into the passage.
7. Never reject an answer. If it is clearly wrong, ask, "Which verse led you to that conclusion?" Or let the group handle the problem by asking them what they think about the question.
8. Avoid going off on tangents. If people wander off course, gently bring them back to the passage being considered.
9. Conclude your time together with conversational prayer. Ask God to help you apply those things that you learned in the session.
10. End on time. This will be easier if you control the pace of the discussion by not spending too much time on some questions or too little on others.

We encourage all small group leaders to use *Leading Life-Changing Small Groups* (Zondervan) by Bill Donahue and the Willow Creek Small Group Team while leading their group. Developed and used by Willow Creek Community Church, this guide is an excellent resource for training and equipping followers of Christ to effectively lead small groups. It includes valuable information on how to utilize fun and creative relationship-building exercises for your group; how to plan your meeting; how to share the leadership load by identifying, developing, and working with an "apprentice leader"; and how to find creative ways to do group prayer. In addition, the book includes material and tips on handling potential conflicts and difficult personalities, forming group covenants, inviting new members, improving listening skills, studying the Bible, and much more. Using *Leading Life-Changing Small Groups* will help you create a group that members love to be a part of.

Now let's discuss the different elements of this small group study guide and how to use them for the session portion of your group meeting.

THE BIG PICTURE

Each session will begin with a short story or overview of the lesson theme. This is called "The Big Picture" because it introduces the central theme of the session. You will need to read this section as a group or have group members read it on their own before discussion begins. Here are three ways you can approach this section of the small group session:

- As the group leader, read this section out loud for the whole group and then move into the questions in the next section, "A Wide Angle View." (You might read the first week, but then use the other two options below to encourage group involvement.)
- Ask a group member to volunteer to read this section for the group. This allows another group member to participate. It is best to ask someone in advance to give them time to read over the section before reading it to the group. It is also good to ask someone to volunteer, and not to assign this task. Some people do not feel comfortable reading in front of a group. After a group member has read this section out loud, move into the discussion questions.
- Allow time at the beginning of the session for each person to read this section silently. If you do this, be sure to allow enough time for everyone to finish reading so they can think about what they've read and be ready for meaningful discussion.

A WIDE ANGLE VIEW

This section includes one or more questions that move the group into a general discussion of the session topic. These questions are designed to help group members begin discussing the topic in an open and honest manner. Once the topic of the lesson has been established, move on to the Bible passage for the session.

A BIBLICAL PORTRAIT

This portion of the session includes a Scripture reading and one or more questions that help group members see how the theme of the session is rooted and based in biblical teaching. The Scripture reading can be handled just like "The Big Picture" section: You can read it for the group, have a group member read it, or allow time for silent reading. Make sure everyone has a Bible or that you have Bibles available for those who need them. Once you have read the passage, ask the question(s) in this section so that group members can dig into the truth of the Bible.

SHARPENING THE FOCUS

The majority of the discussion questions for the session are in this section. These questions are practical and help group members apply biblical teaching to their daily lives.

SNAPSHOTS

The "Snapshots" in each session help prepare group members for discussion. These anecdotes give additional insight to the topic being discussed. Each "Snapshot" should be read at a designated point in the session. This is clearly marked in the session as well as in the Leader's Notes. Again, follow the same format as you do with "The Big Picture" section and the "Biblical Portrait" section: Either you read the anecdote, have a group member volunteer to read, or provide time for silent reading. However you approach this section, you will find these anecdotes very helpful in triggering lively dialogue and moving discussion in a meaningful direction.

PUTTING YOURSELF IN THE PICTURE

Here's where you roll up your sleeves and put the truth into action. This portion is very practical and action-oriented. At the end of each session there will be suggestions for one or two ways group members can put what they've just learned into practice. Review the action goals at the end of each session and challenge group members to work on one or more of them in the coming week.

You will find follow-up questions for the "Putting Yourself in the Picture" section at the beginning of the next week's session. Starting with the second week, there will be time set aside at the beginning of the session to look back and talk about how you have tried to apply God's Word in your life since your last time together.

PRAYER

You will want to open and close your small group with a time of prayer. Occasionally, there will be specific direction within a session for how you can do this. Most of the time, however, you will need to decide the best place to stop and pray. You may want to pray or have a group member volunteer to begin the lesson with a prayer. Or you might want to read "The Big Picture" and discuss the "Wide Angle View" questions before opening in prayer. In some cases, it might be best to open in prayer after you have read the Bible passage. You need to decide where you feel an opening prayer best fits for your group.

When opening in prayer, think in terms of the session theme and pray for group members (including yourself) to be responsive to the truth of Scripture and the working of the Holy Spirit. If you have seekers in your group (people investigating Christianity but not yet believers), be sensitive to your expectations for group prayer. Seekers may not yet be ready to take part in group prayer.

Be sure to close your group with a time of prayer as well. One option is for you to pray for the entire group. Or you might allow time for group members to offer audible prayers that others can agree with in their hearts. Another approach would be to allow a time of silence for one-on-one prayers with God and then to close this time with a simple "Amen."

THE ROAD TO BLESSEDNESS

PSALM 1

INTRODUCTION

Psalm 1 is called "the preface psalm." It contrasts the way of a righteous or a godly person and the way of a wicked or ungodly person. The psalmist claims that certain people are going to experience what the Bible calls blessedness. Blessedness doesn't require any particular circumstances; it transcends circumstances. These are moments we realize with profound clarity that God has filled and satisfied our soul. Blessedness in relationships, for example, are those unforgettable family joys that come in the midst of everyday life. We experience family blessedness sitting around a table and looking around at kids who are laughing, eating, and enjoying themselves. In that moment, we want to take a snapshot and lock it away in our heart . . . we realize how blessed we are.

Blessedness is also discovered in moments of fellowship with Christian brothers and sisters. This can happen while riding in a car, or while running with someone, or during lunch out with a friend. God is present through His Holy Spirit and those "ordinary" moments become sacred, treasured, blessed. And finally, there are those moments of blessedness when there is a miraculous answer to prayer, or when there is a mysterious, yet unmistakable presence of the Holy Spirit. In these moments we find ourselves saying, "I am a totally satisfied man or woman. I am most blessed." This is the message of Psalm 1!

THE BIG PICTURE

Take time to read this introduction with the group. There are suggestions for how this can be done in the beginning of the leader's section.

A WIDE ANGLE VIEW

Question One Spirituality is a hot topic today! People are looking in all sorts of directions in an effort to find out what their future holds. As a group, identify some of the popular sources people seek to discern the future. Have the group picture a friend or relative who is preoccupied with some popular method of figuring out the future.

A Biblical Portrait

Read Psalm 1

Question Two This psalm states that a blessed person is like a tree growing by a river. The psalmist was writing to people who lived in the parched, desert climate of the Middle East. In that part of the world, these words conveyed the idea of an oasis in a desert. Picture a healthy green tree with an unlimited supply of water flowing to its roots, because it is planted by a flowing river. This never-ending river gushes out of the ground in an arid wasteland. What a secure, refreshing picture!

This reminds me of what Jesus said when He was talking with the woman at the well in John 4:14. He told her that when we are rightly related to God through Jesus Christ, the Holy Spirit is like a well of living water springing up from the inside of us. Whatever else we do, buy, or experience, will grow old and run dry, but when we are rightly related to Him, we experience blessedness—a well springing up in our soul that never runs dry. God's mercies are new every morning.

Question Three The psalmist states that the road to barrenness is paved with arrogance and disobedience to God. Those who persist in their self-sufficiency will end up reaping what they have sown for a lifetime—they will be blown away like chaff in the wind. This is an agricultural image. In Old Testament times, after the wheat was crushed and the edible portion was taken out, the worthless chaff was left to blow away.

This image is compounded when we read that the future of these people is judgment and exclusion from the assembly of the righteous. Those who are living out of fellowship with God may have a barren existence here on earth, but their eternities will be even more barren.

Our response to these words should not be one of self-righteous pride that we have a blessed life. We should be filled with concern for those who are heading for a Christless eternity. We should be driven to our knees in prayer and moved to tell them about the blessedness they can find in Jesus.

SHARPENING THE FOCUS

Read Snapshot "Blessedness" before Question 4

Question Four Verse one of this psalm tells us that the blessed person does not walk in the counsel of the wicked or stand in the path of sinners or sit in the seat of scoffers. Let's expand on this imagery.

As a follower of Christ, when you are at the point of making a critical and life-transforming decision, the inclination of your heart is to choose the road of obedience that promises to lead to a future of blessedness. You have read Scripture and you understand that the road of obedience will lead to blessedness beyond description now and forever, and you want this kind of a life. While at this crossroad, people start lining up to give you free advice and counsel. They start casually informing you that the road of obedience does *not* lead to blessedness. They tell you that this road actually leads to bondage, to narrow-mindedness, to an absence of fulfillment. They insist that obedience to God will lead to straight-jacket living.

They say everything they can to keep you off the road of obedience that leads to blessedness. If you are honest about it, you have to admit that some of their counsel sounds good to you. They say "Live for the day! You can have it all and you can have it now! Eat drink and be merry! You only live once, so grab all the gusto you can get! Nice guys finish last! Do unto others before they do unto you!"

We all get this kind of bad advice. The key is to identify where it is coming from and to learn how to ignore it rather than following the counsel of the wicked and suffering for it. We need to stay on the path of obedience and walk in blessedness. As a group, identify various voices and sources of bad counsel and commit yourselves to ignore them!

Question Five We all need to keep our lives rooted in the streams of living water that flow from the heart of God. We need to meet with God on a daily basis to communicate with Him in prayer and to learn from Him through reading the Bible. Encourage group members to communicate how they are making time for personal spiritual growth. Also, seek to develop lines of accountability between group members to support each other in growing deep roots in faith.

Question Six Blessedness carries with it the idea of usefulness and productiveness; a blessed person is a person who bears the fruit of character growth. Blessed people can look back a year or two and rejoice that they can see significant spiritual growth in their life. They can say, "Two years ago I would have responded inappropriately in that circumstance, but I am not that person anymore . . . I have grown." These people discover the bliss of service. They know that being useful and productive for God intensifies feelings of blessedness. Take time as a small group and identify how different members are experiencing fruit growing in their lives as they stay rooted in Christ.

Read Snapshot "Barrenness" before Question 7

Questions Seven & Eight When we see someone living a barren life without Christ, our hearts should be moved. Because we know indescribable blessedness, and know that we matter to God, our response should be one of deep concern and compassion for those who are living a barren existence and face an eternity without Christ. Reflect on these two questions and identify ways you can communicate to others the great blessedness God wants them to experience.

Read Snapshot "The Road to Blessedness . . . Obedience" before Question 9

Question Nine If you make the right choices and stay on the right road, blessedness is guaranteed to you. I don't know about you, but that motivates me toward obedience. Every day there are hundreds of chances to decide what path we will walk. When I face those practical, everyday choices to be honest or tell a lie, I feel the challenge to walk the road marked obedience. It is not always easy, but it leads to blessedness.

When I am thinking and praying about my relationship with Lynne, the Holy Spirit encourages me to take the road of obedience and to be a servant to her. I hear God's call to be encouraging, kind, inspirational, and affirming. When I have an opportunity to do that, but decide instead to be critical, demanding, detached, or arrogant, I walk the road of disobedience. While it is a daily battle to stay on the right road and serve my wife, I know the end result will be blessedness.

Take time as a group to identify those areas where you struggle with staying on the right road. Commit to pray for each other, to encourage each other, and to keep each other accountable. This might also be a good time to reinforce the importance of confidentiality of information communicated in your small group.

PUTTING YOURSELF IN THE PICTURE

Let the group members know you will be providing time at the beginning of the next meeting for them to discuss how they have put their faith into action. Let them tell about how they have acted on one of the two options above. However, don't limit their interaction to these two options. They may have put themselves into the picture in some other way as a result of your study. Allow for honest and open communication.

Also, be clear that there will not be any kind of a "test" or forced reporting. All you are going to do is allow time for people to volunteer to talk about how they have applied what they learned in your last study. Some group members will feel pressured if they think you are going to make everyone report on how they acted on these action goals. You don't want anyone to skip the next group because they are afraid of having to say they did not follow up on what they learned from the prior session. The key is to provide a place for honest communication without creating pressure and fear of being embarrassed.

Every session from this point on will open with a look back at the "Putting Yourself in the Picture" section of the previous session.

PEOPLE MATTER TO GOD

PSALM 8

INTRODUCTION

Too often we feel insignificant and unimportant. The universe is so big and we are so little. In this psalm, David deals with these feelings. He acknowledges that we can feel small in the scope of all of God's creation. But then he turns the tables, elevating human beings to the high place God intended for us. We are made in the image of God, and we matter more to Him than words can describe. In addition, God shows no partiality. He loves us no matter what our skin color, income, or physical beauty. That we matter to God is proven by His sending His only Son to die on the cross as the payment for our sins. This session will be a powerful reminder of just how much we matter to God.

THE BIG PICTURE

Take time to read this introduction with the group. There are suggestions for how this can be done in the beginning of the leader's section.

A WIDE ANGLE VIEW

Question One David is playing a little trick on his readers. He knows where he is going from the beginning of the psalm, but he begins by focusing on our feelings of insignificance. In light of all the created order, we seem so small. However, before the psalm is through, he has done a 180-degree turn. This psalm is not about our insignificance after all, but about the high place every human being has. We matter to God and He loves us. For this psalm to have its full impact, however, it is important to follow David down the road and acknowledge the feelings of insignificance we all face. Once we have done this, we are ready to hear the good news of how significant we are to God.

A BIBLICAL PORTRAIT

Read Psalm 8

Question Two David begins this psalm with a praise attack. He is looking at the wonder of the created order and just has to lift up his voice in praise. David declares that the earth could never contain God's glory, so it overflowed into deep space, extending to the infinite ranges of the universe! David is saying that there is a range of God's glory that extends from the simple to the complex, from the hearts and mouths of mere babes to the infinite reaches of space.

Question Three David begins by focusing on the insignificance and smallness we all feel, then cleverly introduces a turn in his whole line of logic. In verse four we are tempted to think that because of the size and the splendor of God's created realm, humankind isn't very important. We are just puny, little, insignificant specks of flesh. But in verses 5–8, David says that out of the vast array of all that God has created, He has chosen to make people the objects of his affection.

David asks, "Can you believe it? God created all kinds of exotic animals, majestic mountain peaks, endless rivers shimmering with beauty, infinite galaxies, and fathomless ocean depths, and yet we are the apple of His eye. He could have chosen anything out all of the vastness of His created realm to focus His affection and love on, but He picked us."

SHARPENING THE FOCUS

Read Snapshot "Made in the Image of God" before Question 4

Question Four Throughout history, theologians and philosophers have tried to define what it means to be made in the image of God. My goal in these leader's notes is not to be exhaustive, but to highlight some of what it means to be created in God's image.

First, human beings share a portion of God's attributes. Theologians refer to incommunicable and communicable attributes of God. Incommunicable attributes of God are those characteristics of God which are totally unique to God alone. Some of these are God's self-existence (He has no beginning and no one made Him), immutability (He never changes), omnipresence (He can be all places at all times), omnipotence (He can do all things), and many others. These are aspects of God that are reserved for Him alone. Human beings do not have these characteristics and never will.

Communicable attributes of God are characteristics that are bestowed upon mankind to a limited degree. These are characteristics like wisdom, rational thought, goodness, justice, truthfulness, freedom of will, and the list goes on and on. Only human beings have the capacity to resemble God in these ways. We alone bear His likeness.

Second, being made in His image means we have a soul that yearns to be in fellowship with God the Creator. Only human beings reflect on the condition of their relationship to God. Human beings ask questions like, "What is life about? Where am I heading? Where did I come from? If a God exists, how do I relate to Him?" Human beings, because they are made in the image of God, have a soul that longs to be rightly related to Him.

Third, being made in the image of God means human beings are capable of being redeemed. Not even the angels fall into this category. Jesus shed His blood for people. We are the only ones for whom Christ died.

Fourth, only human beings are capable of carrying on God's redemptive purposes. We are singled out of all creation to participate with God in the high calling of telling others they matter to God. Our purpose in life is not to make money, have a good time, buy a nice house, travel the world, or win the praise of people. The highest calling anybody can have is to share in God's endeavor to redeem the rest of mankind. This is something reserved for human beings.

Fifth, only human beings live on into eternity. There is no indication in Scripture that anything else will exist forever. Heaven and earth will go up in smoke, but people remain. Their eternal position will be either with the Lord in the new heaven, or in hell, separated from God forever. This reality shows us just how high the stakes are.

Question Five If all people are made in God's image, we should treat everyone with dignity. There is no room for either racism or sexism in the heart of a follower of Christ. We must reach out to all those who are lost because they matter to God and they should matter to us. If we can't see people through God's eyes, we will be poisoned by prejudice and fail to treat all people with the dignity and love God requires.

Read Snapshot "God Shows No Partiality" before Question 6

Questions Six & Seven Even when we know we have been made in the image of God, we can still feel unimportant. Many things in our culture, our family dynamics, and our own hearts make us feel insignificant. The devil attacks us, telling us we are worthless. Amid all of these attacks, we need to remember that God shows no partiality. He loves us and proved it by paying the ultimate price—the life of His only beloved Son.

Read Snapshot "God Gives Us Responsibility" before Question 8

Question Eight God has given us all responsibilities. As we fulfill His call on our lives, we grow in a sense of our importance to Him. This does not mean He loves us more, but we do get a deeper experience of His love. Learning to serve God, His people, and the world will help each of us understand how much we matter to God.

PUTTING YOURSELF IN THE PICTURE

Challenge group members to take time in the coming week to use part or all of this application section as an opportunity for continued growth.

REASONS FOR PRAISE

PSALM 34

INTRODUCTION

In Psalm 34 David lists several reasons to give praise to God. He seems almost out of control. He can't stop himself. He has to tell anyone who will listen that "God is good!" David praises God for being deeply personal. He is overwhelmed that God, the Creator of heaven and earth, is still interested in David's life. God's goodness and love are available to anyone who will taste and receive Him.

This psalm cries out to a whole new generation of readers. If you have tasted the goodness of God, let your heart erupt in an explosion of exaltation for His goodness. If you don't yet have faith, simply taste of God's goodness. Once you do, you will never want to go picking through the trash heaps of life for food. God has prepared a table of goodness. You are invited to come and dine.

THE BIG PICTURE

Take time to read this introduction with the group. There are suggestions for how this can be done in the beginning of the leader's section.

A WIDE ANGLE VIEW

Question One Many members of your group will have stories to tell that may shock and amaze you. It is startling to discover how many people have had near-death experiences. Most group members who have not had this kind of experience will know someone close to them that has. Encourage the telling of these stories as well as expression of the feelings that followed this near-death experience.

A BIBLICAL PORTRAIT

Read Psalm 34

Questions Two & Three David faced the possibility of death on many occasions. When he was trapped in the city of Gath and pretended to be insane, he barely escaped with his life. In this psalm about deliverance, David may have been thinking about God's deliverance in that situation. He may also have been thinking about the other times he made it through close brushes with death. He desired to express this thanks that God had been so good to him.

We all have life experiences that lead us to praise as we remember God's deliverance, His provision, and His expressions of love. Take time as a group to search this psalm and discover the various expressions of praise that came from the heart of David. Also, seek to identify how this psalm gains deeper meaning when you read it in the context of David's deliverance from the King of Gath.

SHARPENING THE FOCUS

Read Snapshot "An Explosion of Exaltation" before Question 4

Question Four As David reflected on the miracle of God's deliverance, he said, "I want to bless the Lord at all times for what He has done for me. I want blessings to be coming out of my mouth all day and all night. I want His praises to be continually in my mouth. I want to be a nonstop worshiper. I want my soul to boast only in the Lord. I never want to brag about my abilities or my good fortune. I only and always want to boast in the goodness of God." Can you hear the intensity in his voice and the cry of His heart?

David also expressed his desire to hear his voice joined by others who would give praise and worship to God. I think I can identify with David's heart on this matter. I was at a football game at the University of Michigan in Ann Arbor, Michigan, some years ago. There were over 104,000 people gathered. During the game I found myself thinking, *What if all these voices were singing "How Great Thou Art." Wouldn't that be something?* Then I thought about what the book of Revelation says, that someday all believers from all ages are going to join with the tens of thousands of angels and all of us together are going to worship God. What a thrill that is going to be! This is the heart of David. He longed to hear everyone lift their voices in praise.

Read Snapshot "The Power of Personal Faith" before Question 6

Question Six When God speaks to us or when the Holy Spirit gives His promptings, we must decide if we will respond. It takes spiritual courage to make that leap of faith and follow Him even when we are fearful. At this point, we choose to let God be our lifeline and to trust in Him alone. These are the moments during which our character is formed, our faith is deepened, and we learn how good our God really is.

Each time we trust God as He leads by His Spirit, He proves Himself trustworthy. Pretty soon, over a period of time, we begin to build a faith portfolio—a personal scrapbook of God's rescues, miracles, deliverances, and answers to prayer. After enough of these experiences, we begin to believe God instead of just believe *in* God. We start to naturally exercise personal demonstrations of faith. These experiences, in turn, create deeper confidence in God, boldness in life, vitality in prayer, and enthusiasm in worship.

Read Snapshot "An Invitation to Anyone" before Question 8

Questions Eight & Nine David wasn't afraid to give an open invitation to anybody. He was saying, "Taste and see. Anybody who can hear my voice, taste and see that the Lord is good. God will prove Himself to be a good God. As you taste and experience the goodness of God in your own life, you will come to believe." David was able to be very specific as he listed all the ways he had experienced God's goodness.

This psalm is a great example for us. We need to learn how to list all of the ways we have experienced God's goodness. If we honestly reflect on how God has worked in our lives, we should be able to go on for hours telling others how we have tasted the goodness of the Lord. In addition, we need to invite them to taste God's goodness for themselves. We can invite them to read the Bible or encourage them to begin praying and asking God to show Himself in their lives. We can invite them to a worship service, a seekers' event, or a Christian concert. Ultimately, we invite them into the life Jesus offers. Evangelism is no more complicated than telling others about the goodness of God we have experienced, and inviting them to taste God's goodness in their own lives.

PUTTING YOURSELF IN THE PICTURE

Challenge group members to take time in the coming week to use part or all of this application section as an opportunity for continued growth.

GOD ONLY

PSALM 62

INTRODUCTION

I regularly get mail from people who beg me to warn our church members to learn from their mistakes. Someone will write to me and say something like, "Tell the people in the church never to take their first drink," and then they write six or seven pages describing the disastrous consequences of alcoholism. "Never marry an unbeliever" is another one. "Never smoke that first joint." "Don't get reckless with credit cards." The list goes on and on. I once received a letter from a woman who pleaded with me to tell all other women to never get an abortion. She wrote three or four pages describing the agony she had gone through since she had one. The truth is, we have all learned lessons the hard way and wish others could avoid the same pain.

In this session we will hear David teach us a lesson he learned from personal experience. At one point, David was completely committed to God. He was a "God only" man. Nothing mattered more to him than serving God and he let nothing stand in the way of being a man after God's heart. But then he began to waver. He allowed other pursuits and loves to creep in and take over his heart and life. He became a "God and" man. He loved God, but he was also in love with wealth, power, political maneuvering, women, and fame. The little shepherd boy had become a national hero and had ascended to the throne of Israel. He had moved up in the eyes of the world, but his affections were divided. Through this, David learned some hard lessons. Through this psalm he tells us, "Don't fall into the trap of becoming a 'God and' man or woman . . . Be a 'God only' person!"

THE BIG PICTURE

Take time to read this introduction with the group. There are suggestions for how this can be done in the beginning of the leader's section.

A WIDE ANGLE VIEW

Question One We have all learned lessons the hard way. Some stories might be very humorous and some might be very painful. Encourage group members to tell their stories of how they learned a life lesson the hard way.

A BIBLICAL PORTRAIT

Read Psalm 62

Question Two The heart of this psalm is the contrast between two phrases: "God only" and "God and." You see, David's life changed drastically after his confrontation with Goliath. He experienced a meteoric rise to national attention. In a relatively short period of time, he went from being an unknown, deeply spiritual shepherd boy to a national folk hero. He went from tending sheep to becoming heir to the throne. Finally, David became the King of Israel.

My hunch is that while David was an unknown shepherd boy, he spent the beautiful, starlit evenings playing his musical instrument and worshiping God. During those years David was a "God only" man. His heart was in harmony with the heart of God. His mind was fixed on God. His worship flowed freely heavenward.

It is after his rise to fame and after learning some tough lessons in the school of hard knocks that David invites his listeners to be "God only" people. He had walked the "God and" road and knew it was a dead end. This psalm lists many areas where we need to be sure we keep God on the throne.

Question Three David gives some serious warnings as well as hope-filled promises. Have group members paraphrase these in the space provided in their books. Invite them to read their versions of these warning and promises and explain what they think David means.

SHARPENING THE FOCUS

Read Snapshot "God Only" before Question 4

Question Four "God only" people know that the only source of ultimate love, inner strength, and justice is God. There are those who have learned that being sold out for God is the only way to go. God is first in their life and rules supreme in their heart. It shows in their attitudes, their words, and their actions. If you have a handful of "God only" Christians in your life, be thankful. These people are an inspiration and a gift from God!

Questions Five & Six We all have areas of our lives we can offer more completely to God. Spend time as a group communicating one area in which you need to be more sold out for God and in which you need to become a "God only" follower of Christ. Commit to pray for each other and to be aggressive in keeping each other accountable in this specific area of your life.

Read Snapshot "God and . . ." before Question 7

Question Seven I can't help but think when I read verses 9 and 10 in this psalm that David is saying to his listeners, "I have learned some lessons from the school of hard knocks. I have walked through some painful—even embarrassing—experiences. Learn from me. Listen to me. These are lessons I learned through getting burned." David, writing with his own blood, so to speak, lists a few consequences of living this kind of a life.

One lesson David wants us to learn is that living to impress other people is a dead-end road. Applause from others isn't what it is cracked up to be. Even though David defeated Goliath and was ushered into the city as a hero, it hurt him in the long run. The multitudes sang his praises. It felt great to be the object of everyone's attention and affection. But slowly and surely, his fame and popularity changed him from being a "God only" man into a "God and" man.

David also teaches us another lesson. He was content and satisfied with the small income of a shepherd. But when he became king, money started to roll in. He had access to an enormous amount of wealth. Instead of drawing him closer to God, this made him a "God and" man. Slowly but surely, his security moved from trust in God to trust in "God and his treasure chest." At long last, David learned that no person can serve two masters. God must rule in our lives, and only God.

Question Eight This is the opposite side of the coin we looked at in question five. You have talked about what stands in the way of group members being "God only" people. This question will lead to honest communication of one area where group members are putting something ahead of God. Encourage group members to identify these things and to seek the support of other group members. Also note that the second section of the "Putting Yourself in the Picture" section at the end of the lesson will help group members in this process of moving from being "God and" Christians to "God only" followers of Christ.

Putting Yourself in the Picture

Challenge group members to take time in the coming week to use part or all of this application section as an opportunity for continued growth.

FREEDOM FROM FEAR

PSALM 91

INTRODUCTION

None of us is exempt from fears. Sometimes these fears are small pestering fears that bother us but don't keep us awake at night. At other times they are pressing fears that create stress and anxiety. There are also major-league fears that paralyze us and come crashing into our lives unannounced and uninvited. No matter what fears we face, we need to discover the freedom God promises. We must not be enslaved by fear.

In this session we will look at three keys to freedom from fear. The writer of Psalm 91 offers practical insight for how we can be set free from the bondage of fear. First, we need to know the character of the God we serve. He is a mighty God who is able and willing to deliver us. Knowing His character helps set us free from fear. Second, the psalmist reminds us that God has sent angels to watch over us and protect us. This also helps set us free from fear. And third, we are told that God hears our prayers and our cries. We are released from the grip of fear when we know God hears and answers our prayers. God does not want us to live in fear, but in freedom.

THE BIG PICTURE

Take time to read this introduction with the group. There are suggestions for how this can be done in the beginning of the leader's section.

A WIDE ANGLE VIEW

Question One We all have stories to tell about how we have dealt with fear in our lives. Invite group members to share on any level they feel comfortable. Some will dive right into deeper levels of fear and others will stay with small, pestering fears. The goal is to open up honest communication about the various fears members of your group have lived with in the past and still confront today.

A BIBLICAL PORTRAIT

Read Psalm 91

Question Two The psalmist, especially in verse 3 and then in verses 5, 6, and 7, seems to be making the point that he understands why some of us wrestle with various levels of fear. He realizes that at some time in every person's life random strikes of adversity and tragedy come crashing in. He is addressing the natural human tendency to wonder when the lightning is going to strike. In an effort to help us understand that fear does not need to rule our lives, the psalmist paints pictures of the character of God. These images help us grow more courageous.

In verse 3 the psalmist refers to the fowler's snare. In those days, bird trappers would install a net with weights in the limbs of a tree and then sprinkle seeds under that tree. When a flock of birds would come to eat the seed, they would cut the rope, and the weighted net would fall over the flock of birds, trapping them. They would struggle to get free, but there was no hope of escape. This picture teaches us that God will come along and set us free, even after we have been trapped.

In verse 5 the psalmist says if you live in the real world for any period of time, you are well-acquainted with some of the terrors that happen at night or midday. Yet in a dangerous world, the psalmist reminds us that we don't have to be afraid. This is not an encouragement to be irresponsibly unsafe; it is simply a reminder that we are never alone. We are secure with our God.

Question Three God wants His children to be optimistic, confident, courageous, and trusting. It grieves the heart of God to see us crippled with fear, incapacitated by anxiety, and immobilized by worry. It is becoming clearer to me, as I mature in the Christian faith, that one of God's main missions is to free us from the debilitating bonds of fear and anxiety. It breaks His heart to see us drained, debilitated, and demoralized by runaway fear.

Psalm 91 inspires each and every one of us to choose a walk of faith and not to cave in to fear. Its portrait of one man who, in spite of all the apparent chaos and uncertainty around him, made the choice to walk in faith and not in fear is an example we all need to learn to follow.

Sharpening the Focus

Read Snapshot "Knowing Who God Is" before Question 4

Question Four Verse 4 reminds us that God is not simply mighty and majestic, He is also tender and personal. He wants to cover and shelter us with His wings. God's character is that of a protecting mother who would never want to see her children hurt. Remember the story of Jesus as He overlooked the city of Jerusalem and finally broke down crying. He was saying to the world, "You think it is safe where you are. You think you are better off on your own, out fending for yourself. But I would love to take all of you and put you under My wing." What a picture of love and care!

The psalmist also says God is almighty, a fortress, a bulwark, and a deliverer. He uses a military example, talking about God's faithfulness as a shield. When we feel vulnerable and exposed, God is our protector. When we feel like an easy target for any stray calamity, we need to remember that He is our shield and fortress. When we know He protects us, wandering in the wastelands of fears makes no sense.

Read Snapshot "Surrounded by Angels" before Question 6

Questions Six & Seven Aside from these passages in Psalms, there is another great story about God's protecting angels. In chapter six of 2 Kings, we read of Elisha the prophet being surrounded by hundreds of enemy troops, who wanted to kill him. Elisha's servant got very fearful as the enemy got closer. He turned to Elisha and said, "What are we going to do?" Elisha responded, "We are going to *fear not.*" Then Elisha said to his servant, "There are more of us than there are of them." The servant had no idea what Elisha was talking about. He saw hundreds of the opposition surrounding them, and he and Elisha were defenseless. Just then, Elisha asked God to open the eyes of his servant so he could see the angels. Elisha's servant looked and saw the entire countryside filled with angelic armies. He and Elisha were surrounded by the enemy, but the enemy was surrounded by the armies of God. Do you get the picture? Elisha could say, "Fear not" because he knew the angels of God were there to protect him. We can live with the same understanding.

Angels surround, protect, guide, guard, and fend off Satan's random attacks. All of us have had close calls in traffic, travel, relational situations, decision-making incidents, and many other kinds of situations. It is very possible there is some angelic involvement in times like those. I would venture to guess that there are hundreds of times when we have each been spared and weren't even aware of it. The psalmist reminds us that we can walk in faith because of who God is and because God has charged His angels to watch over us.

Read Snapshot "The Power of Prayer" before Question 8

Questions Eight & Nine People often come up to me and tell me about problems that are producing high levels of fear in their lives. Sometimes I perceive they don't really want help or advice on some action they can take. They are perfectly content in telling me about the problem, because there is a "pity factor" built-in. They don't want to be set free from fear; they just want some sympathy and attention in the midst of their fear.

When people bring their fears to God in prayer, it can be the same situation. They are informing God about their problems and looking for some comfort, but they don't really want to be set free. In fact, in some cases, they seem to have a need to cling to their fear. When they are finished praying, they get up from their knees and continue to live in the same debilitated fashion as before they were down on their knees praying.

This is not the kind of prayer that releases you from the bonds of fear. When you pray about a problem, remember first of all that God already knows about the problem. As you *tell* God the problem, be sure to *give* God the problem and the fear associated with it. For more help in this area of prayer, see the first section of the "Putting Yourself in the Picture" portion of this study.

Putting Yourself in the Picture

Challenge group members to take time in the coming week to use part or all of this application section as an opportunity for continued growth.

THE GREATNESS OF GOD

PSALM 145

INTRODUCTION

Our enthusiasm for private and corporate worship is directly proportionate to our knowledge and understanding of God. Over the years, I have found myself emphasizing the theme of God's identity more and more in my teaching ministry. I just can't seem to avoid it. Every day I see a little more clearly how almost everything flows out of our understanding of who God is. When we know who God is, we can't refrain from worshiping Him. If we don't know who God is, if we don't understand His character, we can't be coerced into worshiping Him.

It is the same thing with prayer. People who understand the heart of God, His omnipotence, His interest in every little situation of life, are people of prayer. They can't help themselves. And people who don't understand God's power don't pray much.

It is also the same way with telling others about God. People who really are in tune with the heart of God are bold to tell others about Him. They look for opportunities in the marketplace, the neighborhood, and everywhere they go.

This psalm gives us insight into the God we serve. When we see Him clearly, we begin to worship, pray, serve, and tell others, "What a great God we have!" This is the natural response of a Christian who understands the heart and character of God.

THE BIG PICTURE

Take time to read this introduction with the group. There are suggestions for how this can be done in the beginning of the leader's section.

A WIDE ANGLE VIEW

Question One In verses 1 and 2 of Psalm 145 David tells us there is something he is so excited about that he intends to do it every day, forever and ever. "What could it be?" you wonder? Worship! David is so taken with the whole concept of worship and adoration that there isn't much else in his life he would rather do. Remember that David was a regular sort of guy—a warrior, a politician, a husband, a father, a businessman— but he wanted to worship God more than he wanted to do anything else.

What activity or endeavor would you really want to participate in every day? What is it that doesn't get old for you? What is it that never gets boring or predictable? What is it that you engage in that gets deeper and more meaningful as time passes? I hope one of those things is worship. If not, pray for a deeper understanding of God's character so your heart will have a deeper longing to worship.

A BIBLICAL PORTRAIT

Read Psalm 145

Question Two Have group members read this psalm and try to let their heart beat with the heart of David. If they can do this, answering these two questions from his point of view should be deeply meaningful. Too often we read a passage from where we stand. Have group members answer these questions with David's voice. What would he like to do forever? What aspects of God's character cause him to explode in a song of praise?

Question Three Psalm 145 offers great insight to the character of God, the activity of God, and how human beings should respond to God. Take time as a group to list what you learn in each area. This will lay the groundwork and set the stage for the discussion that will follow.

SHARPENING THE FOCUS

Read Snapshot "The Greatness of God" before Question 4

Questions Four & Five Psalm 145:4 says that God proves His greatness through mighty acts. One generation of people will rejoice in telling the next generation how wonderful God is. One generation will have so many answers to prayer, so many miracles, so many daring rescues, so many last-minute provisions, so many unwarranted blessings and surprises, so many reconciliations, that they just have to let their hearts spill over as they tell the next generation about the greatness of God.

We have all seen God's greatness. Now we have to learn how to tell others. What better place to start this habit than in the safety of your small group? Communicate the various ways you have seen God reveal His greatness in a general sense. Then, get more specific. Describe how you have experienced the amazing power of God's greatness in your own life. This is not bragging or boasting; it is simply telling your story of experiencing God's greatness. Rejoice as one generation tells the next about God's mighty greatness.

This may sound strange at first, but it is important to invite God to reveal His greatness in us. I find it necessary to invite God, on a regular basis, to be great in me. God is great and He wants to do great things through His children. We just need to be open for Him to use us. In the course of the day we need to say, "God, You are a great God, but I often doubt You can be great in me. I often doubt You can do great things *through* me. But here I am. If You want to do something through my life today, I am available."

Read Snapshot "The Goodness of God" before Question 6

Questions Six & Seven It is important for us to live in a way that God is free to express the full measure of His goodness to us. A good God can and will chastise His children in love when they need it. But at the same time, our God pours out overflowing goodness into the lives of His children. Every good gift we have in life comes from His hand. Use this opportunity to celebrate how God has poured His good gifts into the lives of your small group members. Doing this will also give perspective for those who live with the sense that God's goodness is going to run out some day. When we look back and see His constant outpouring of good things, we can trust Him for the future.

Read Snapshot "The Glory of God" before Question 8

Question Eight In Isaiah 6 God revealed His glory. As a leader, it might be helpful to read this chapter before your group meets. Isaiah had a vision about the glory of God. In the vision there is thunder, quaking, smoke, angels, and an overwhelming sense of the glory of God. Isaiah is overcome with his own sense of sinfulness and inadequacy. In the presence of the glory of God, every knee bows.

Sometimes when my wife, Lynne, and I go on summer vacation we just sit and watch a glorious sunset. At other times we have watched a powerful thunderstorm or traveled to places where there are majestic mountain peaks. Often we have said to each other, "That's nothing compared to the glory of God. The One who made all of this loves us. We matter to Him!"

Read Snapshot "The Grace of God" before Question 9

Questions Nine & Ten Take time as a group to express how you have experienced God's amazing grace. Also, be creative in how you can declare your praise for His grace. Think on both a personal and a group level. How can we respond to this great God who has poured out His grace on His children?

PUTTING YOURSELF IN THE PICTURE

Challenge group members to take time in the coming week to use part or all of this application section as an opportunity for continued growth.

ADDITIONAL WILLOW CREEK RESOURCES

Small Group Resources

Coaching Life-Changing Small Group Leaders, by Bill Donahue and Greg Bowman
The Complete Book of Questions, by Garry Poole
The Connecting Church, by Randy Frazee
Leading Life-Changing Small Groups, by Bill Donahue and the Willow Creek Team
The Seven Deadly Sins of Small Group Ministry, by Bill Donahue and Russ Robinson
Walking the Small Group Tightrope, by Bill Donahue and Russ Robinson

Evangelism Resources

Becoming a Contagious Christian (book), by Bill Hybels and Mark Mittelberg
The Case for a Creator, by Lee Strobel
The Case for Christ, by Lee Strobel
The Case for Faith, by Lee Strobel
Seeker Small Groups, by Garry Poole
The Three Habits of Highly Contagious Christians, by Garry Poole

Spiritual Gifts and Ministry

Network Revised (training course), by Bruce Bugbee and Don Cousins
The Volunteer Revolution, by Bill Hybels
What You Do Best in the Body of Christ—Revised, by Bruce Bugbee

Marriage and Parenting

Fit to Be Tied, by Bill and Lynne Hybels
Surviving a Spiritual Mismatch in Marriage, by Lee and Leslie Strobel

Ministry Resources

An Hour on Sunday, by Nancy Beach
Building a Church of Small Groups, by Bill Donahue and Russ Robinson
The Heart of the Artist, by Rory Noland
Making Your Children's Ministry the Best Hour of Every Kid's Week, by Sue Miller and David Staal
Thriving as an Artist in the Church, by Rory Noland

Curriculum

An Ordinary Day with Jesus, by John Ortberg and Ruth Haley Barton
Becoming a Contagious Christian (kit), by Mark Mittelberg, Lee Strobel, and Bill Hybels
Good Sense Budget Course, by Dick Towner, John Tofilon, and the Willow Creek Team
If You Want to Walk on Water, You've Got to Get Out of the Boat, by John Ortberg with Stephen and Amanda Sorenson
The Life You've Always Wanted, by John Ortberg with Stephen and Amanda Sorenson
The Old Testament Challenge, by John Ortberg with Kevin and Sherry Harney, Mindy Caliguire, and Judson Poling

WILLOW
Willow Creek Association

Willow Creek Association
Vision, Training, Resources for Prevailing Churches

This resource was created to serve you and to help you build a local church that prevails. It is just one of many ministry tools that are part of the Willow Creek Resources® line, published by the Willow Creek Association together with Zondervan.

The Willow Creek Association (WCA) was created in 1992 to serve a rapidly growing number of churches from across the denominational spectrum that are committed to helping unchurched people become fully devoted followers of Christ. Membership in the WCA now numbers over 10,500 Member Churches worldwide from more than ninety denominations.

The Willow Creek Association links like-minded Christian leaders with each other and with strategic vision, training, and resources in order to help them build prevailing churches designed to reach their redemptive potential. Here are some of the ways the WCA does that.

- **A2: Building Prevailing Acts 2 Churches—Today**—an annual two-and-a-half day event, held at Willow Creek Community Church in South Barrington, Illinois, to explore strategies for building churches that reach out to seekers and build believers, and to discover new innovations and breakthroughs from Acts 2 churches around the country.

- **The Leadership Summit**—a once a year, two-and-a-half-day conference to envision and equip Christians with leadership gifts and responsibilities. Presented live at Willow Creek as well as via satellite broadcast to over one hundred locations across North America, this event is designed to increase the leadership effectiveness of pastors, ministry staff, volunteer church leaders, and Christians in the marketplace.

- **Ministry-Specific Conferences**—throughout each year the WCA hosts a variety of conferences and training events—both at Willow Creek's main campus and offsite, across the U.S., and around the world—targeting church leaders and volunteers in ministry-specific areas such as: evangelism, small groups, preaching and teaching, the arts, children, students, women, volunteers, stewardship, raising up resources, etc.

- **Willow Creek Resources®**—provides churches with trusted and field-tested ministry resources in such areas as leadership, evangelism, spiritual formation, spiritual gifts, small groups, stewardship, student ministry, children's ministry, the use of the arts-drama, media, contemporary music —and more.

- **WCA Member Benefits**—includes substantial discounts to WCA training events, a 20 percent discount on all Willow Creek Resources®, *Defining Moments* monthly audio journal for leaders, quarterly *Willow* magazine, access to a Members-Only section on WillowNet, monthly communications, and more. Member Churches also receive special discounts and premier services through WCA's growing number of ministry partners—Select Service Providers—and save an average of $500 annually depending on the level of engagement.

For specific information about WCA conferences, resources, membership, and other ministry services contact:

Willow Creek Association
P.O. Box 3188
Barrington, IL 60011-3188
Phone: 847-570-9812
Fax: 847-765-5046
www.willowcreek.com

Continue building your new community!
New Community Series
BILL HYBELS AND JOHN ORTBERG
with Kevin and Sherry Harney

Exodus: *Journey Toward God* 0-310-22771-2

Parables: *Imagine Life God's Way* 0-310-22881-6

Sermon on the Mount[1]: *Connect with God* 0-310-22884-0

Sermon on the Mount[2]: *Connect with Others* 0-310-22883-2

Acts: *Build Community* 0-310-22770-4

Romans: *Find Freedom* 0-310-22765-8

Philippians: *Run the Race* 0-310-22766-6

Colossians: *Discover the New You* 0-310-22769-0

James: *Live Wisely* 0-310-22767-4

1 Peter: *Stand Strong* 0-310-22773-9

1 John: *Love Each Other* 0-310-22768-2

Revelation: *Experience God's Power* 0-310-22882-4

Look for New Community at your local Christian bookstore.

Continue the Transformation
Pursuing Spiritual Transformation
JOHN ORTBERG, LAURIE PEDERSON,
AND JUDSON POLING

Grace: *An Invitation to a Way of Life* 0-310-22074-2

Growth: *Training vs. Trying* 0-310-22075-0

Groups: *The Life-Giving Power of Community* 0-310-22076-9

Gifts: *The Joy of Serving God* 0-310-22077-7

Giving: *Unlocking the Heart of Good Stewardship* 0-310-22078-5

Fully Devoted: *Living Each Day in Jesus' Name* 0-310-22073-4

Look for Pursuing Spiritual Transformation at your local Christian bookstore.

TOUGH QUESTIONS
Garry Poole and Judson Poling

Softcover

REALITY CHECK SERIES
by Mark Ashton

God Is Closer Than You Think

John Ortberg

Two works of art help John Ortberg think about the presence of God. One is Michelangelo Buonarroti's brilliant painting of God and Adam on the ceiling of the Sistine Chapel. God is close. His hand comes within a hair's breadth of the hand of the man. It seems to say that God is closer than we think—he's here, now, today, accessible to all who will but "lift a finger."

The second work of art is Martin Hanford's cartoon character Waldo. He is on every page of the Where's Waldo? books, but he can be difficult to find. In the same way, even though God is present on every page of our lives, he's often not easy to spot.

In *God Is Closer Than You Think*, John Ortberg examines this frustrating paradox of the Christian life.

"When it is so easy to 'see' God all around me (in trees, in birds, in nature) why is it so hard to feel his presence—especially when I need him most?"

Ortberg helps readers discover the secret to living daily in the reality of God's most frequent promise in Scripture, "I will be with you."

Hardcover: 0-310-25349-7
ebooks:
Adobe Acrobat eBook Reader® format: 0-310-26336-0
Microsoft Reader® format: 0-310-26337-9
Mobipocket® format: 0-310-26339-5
Palm Reader® format: 0-310-26338-7
Unabridged Audio Pages® CD: 0-310-26379-4
Abridged Audio Pages® CD: 0-310-26450-2

Pick up a copy today at your favorite bookstore!

ZONDERVAN™

GRAND RAPIDS, MICHIGAN 49530 USA

WWW.ZONDERVAN.COM

WILLOW

Willow Creek Association

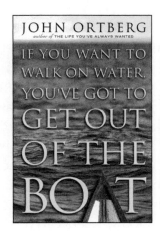

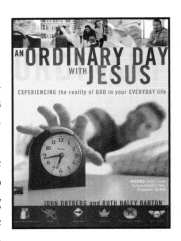
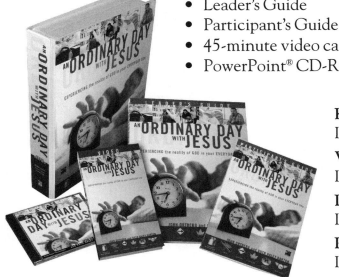